GW01375326

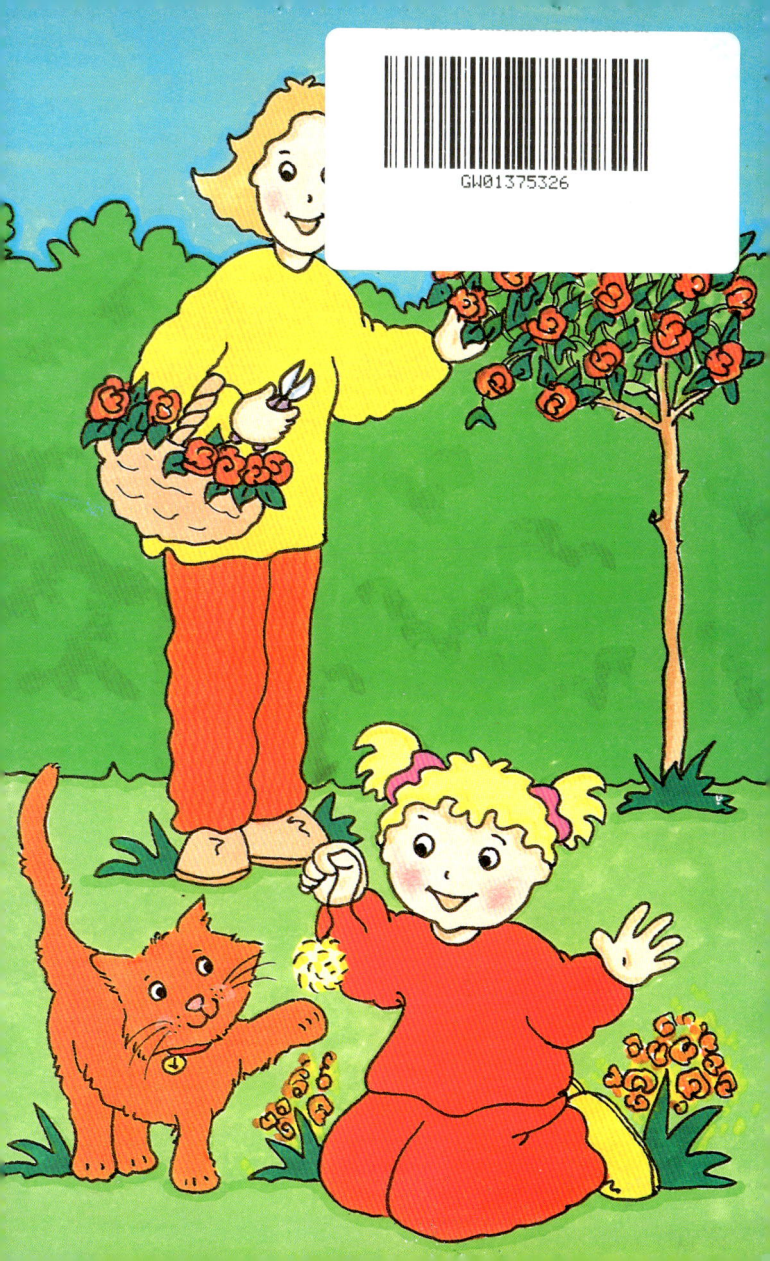

© 1998 Geddes & Grosset Ltd
Published by Geddes & Grosset Ltd,
New Lanark, Scotland.

ISBN 1 85534 842 X

Produced by Simon Girling & Associates,
Hadleigh, Suffolk.

Printed and bound in China.

10 9 8 7 6 5 4 3 2 1

SUSIE & SAM

Visit the Fire Station

GEDDES & GROSSET

Susie and Sam were learning about fire safety at school. A fireman called George had come to talk to their class, and now they were going to visit the fire station with their teacher, Mrs Bonetti.

Mrs Bonetti checked the children's names on her list, then they all climbed into the school bus and off they went.

When the bus stopped outside the fire station, Mrs Bonetti put her finger to her lips. The children quietened down.

"Now, everyone," said Mrs Bonetti, "it is very kind of George to let us come and see the fire station. We must all be on our very best behaviour, mustn't we?"

Susie, Sam and their friends nodded.

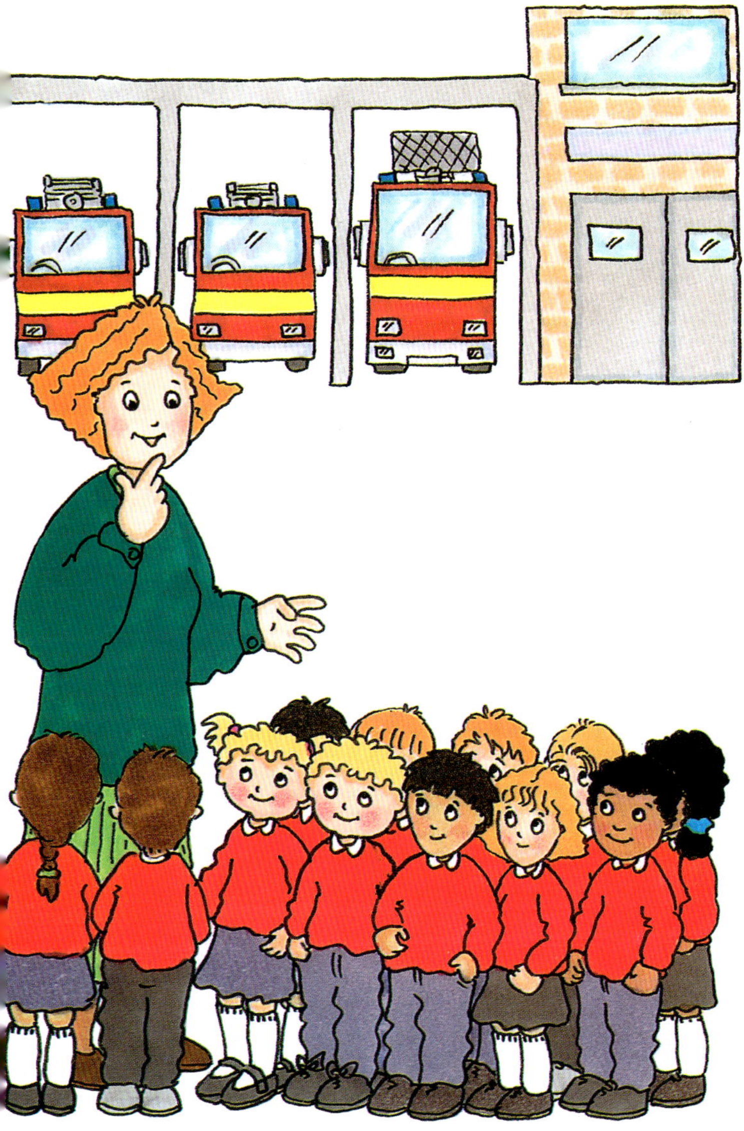

George came out to meet them with a woman dressed in uniform, just like him.

"Children, this is Deborah," said George. "She is going to help me to show you around."

"Are you a fireman too?" asked Sam.

"Women are allowed to be firefighters too, you know!" laughed Deborah.

"How do you become a firefighter?" Susie wanted to know.

"You have to pass lots of tests, and you have to be very strong and fit," said Deborah. "Some of the equipment is very heavy! Come inside, and we'll show you."

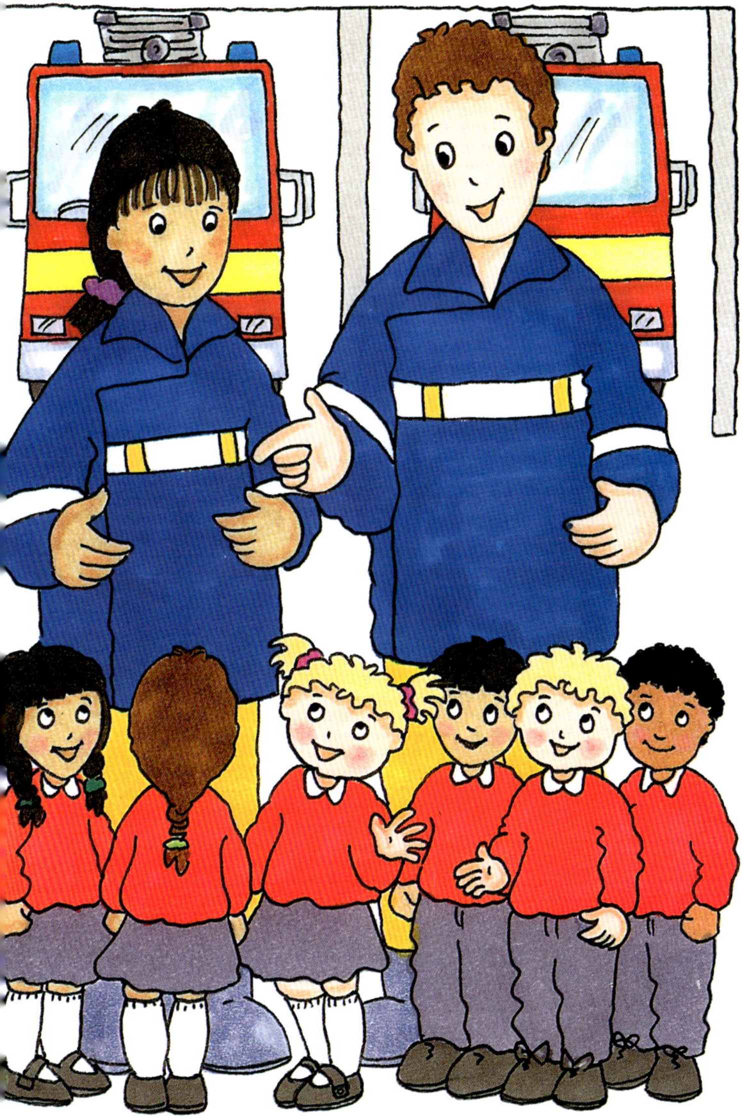

Deborah led the way into the fire station. First they went to look at the fire engines. They were not all the same, but they were all very clean and shiny.

"Who cleans the engines?" asked Afifa.
"We do – it's hard work!" said George.

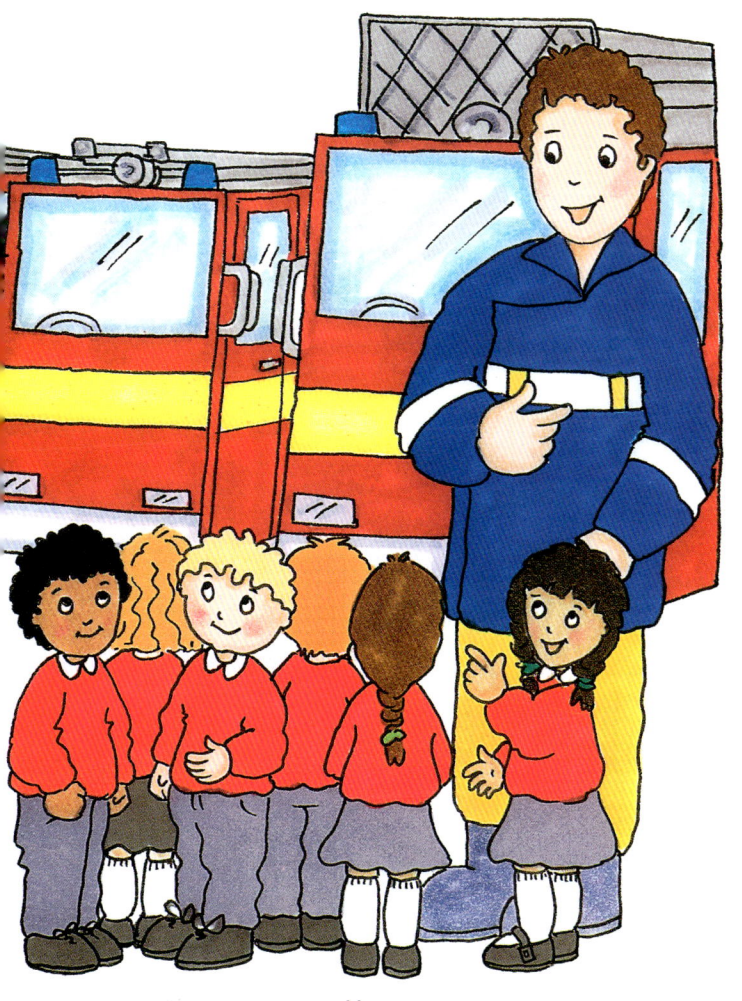

One engine was much bigger than the others.

"I've seen one of those on television," said Ben, Sam's friend. "That thing on top unfolds and can stretch right up to the top of high buildings."

"That's right," said George. "That's the hydraulic platform. We use it for putting out fires in flats or other high buildings."

George and Deborah took the children over to one of the fire engines and let them all climb inside to have a look.

"How does the siren work?" said Sam. "Mind your ears!" said George. He pressed a button. The noise was terrible!

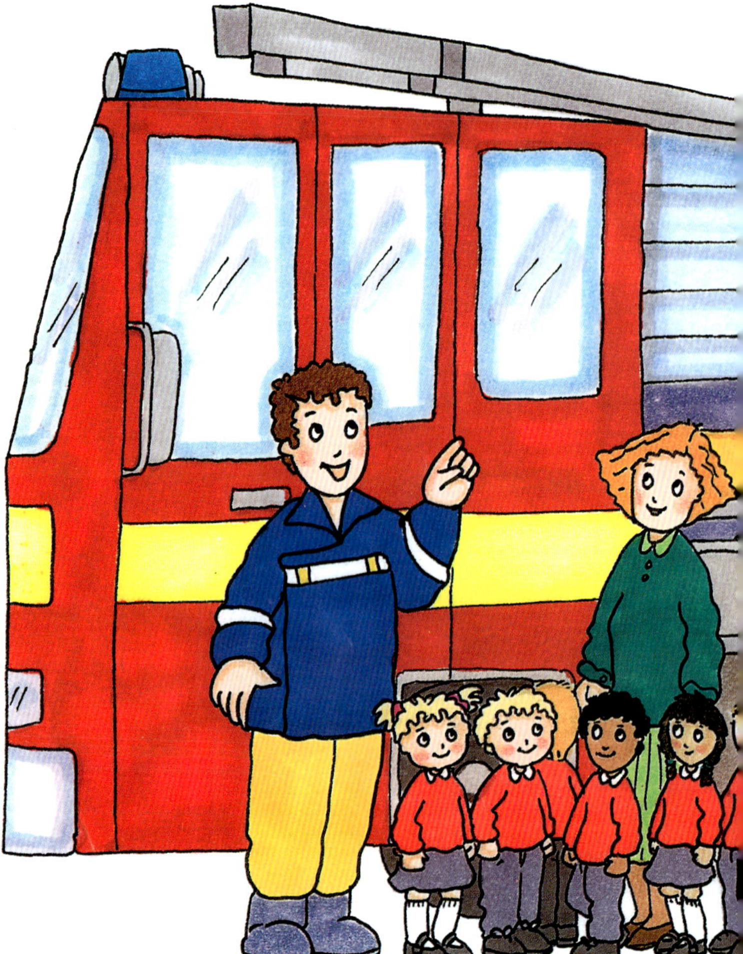

George and Deborah showed the children the hoses curled up on the fire engine, the ladders that they needed and all the other equipment that they used.

The children tried on the helmets, and so did Mrs Bonetti! Deborah showed them how she put on the oxygen cylinder and breathing apparatus that firefighters need to wear in very smoky places. She let the children try to lift one of the oxygen cylinders. It was too heavy!

"Now you see why we have to be strong and fit," she said.

"We have to be tidy as well," she said. "Everything must be put back in exactly the right place so that we can find it when we really need it."

George and Deborah took the children on a tour of the rest of the fire station. Sam particularly liked the look of the pole that the firefighters had to slide down to get to the fire engines in a hurry, but George said that it was too dangerous for the children to try.

Susie liked the dormitory where the firefighters could sleep when they were on night duty.

"How do you wake up in time if there is a fire?" she asked.

"The alarm bell is very loud!" said George.

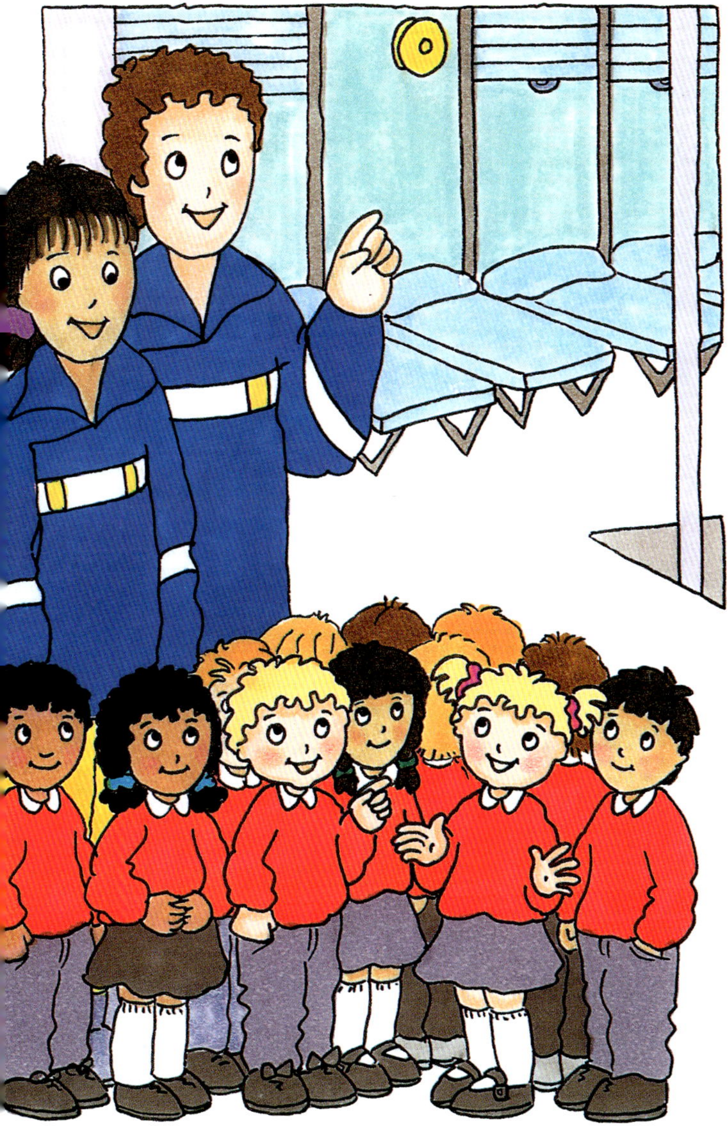

Everything was interesting, but the best bit was yet to come. George and Deborah took the children and Mrs Bonetti up to the canteen for a drink. It was very nice, but it was very empty.

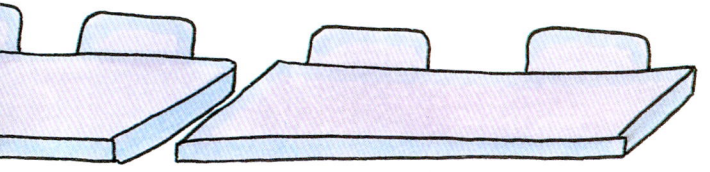

"Where are all the other firefighters?" Sam wanted to know.

"Look out of the window," said George.

From the window, the children could see a big yard. At one end of the yard were two fire engines full of firefighters, dressed in their firefighting gear. At the other end were two big oil drums with flames coming out of them.

"They are doing exercises," said George. "Today they have to see how fast they can unroll their hoses, connect them up and put out the fire. Which team do you think will win?"

The race began, and all the children crowded together at the window, cheering the firefighters on. How fast they were!

The team that Susie and Sam had chosen worked extra hard, and soon their hoses were all connected up.

Two firefighters held on to the hose and aimed it at the oil drum. The water flew out of the end of the hose, putting the fire out in no time at all. It was exciting!

At the end of the visit, Mrs Bonetti and the children said thank you to George and Deborah. When they got back to school they drew some pictures of their visit.

It had been a great day. Susie and Sam couldn't wait to tell Mum and Dad all about it!